The Railroad

INVENTIONS BRING CHANGE

Cameron McRae

PICTURE CREDITS

Cover: railroad poster (1869) © Hulton Archive/Getty Images;
a steam engine at Promontory Point © Wolfgang Kaehler/
Corbis/Tranz.

Photographs: page 1 © Hulton Archive/Getty Images; page 4
(bottom left) © Hulton Archive/Getty Images; page 4 (bottom right)
© Minnesota Historical Society/Corbis/Tranz; page 5 (top)
© Corbis/Tranz; page 5 (bottom left) © Kevin Fleming/Corbis/
Tranz; page 5 (bottom right) © Bettmann/Corbis/Tranz; page 6
© Corbis/Tranz; page 8 © Archive Holdings Inc/Image Bank/Getty
Images; page 9 © Michael Maslan Historic Photographs/Corbis/
Tranz; page 10 © Bettmann/Corbis/Tranz; page 12 © Wolfgang
Kaehler/Corbis/Tranz; page 13 © Hulton Archive/Getty Images;
pages 14–15 © Bettmann/Corbis/Tranz; page 16, Photodisc;
page 21 © Hulton Archive/Getty Images; page 22 © Corbis/Tranz;
page 23 © Historical Picture Archive/Corbis/Tranz; page 24
© Hulton-Deutsch Collection/Corbis/Tranz; page 25 © Hulton
Archive/Getty Images; page 26 © Bettmann/Corbis/Tranz;
page 29 © Mary Kate Denny/Stone/Getty Images.

Illustrations: page 11 by Jamie Laurie; page 19 by Kevin Currie.

Produced through the worldwide resources of the National
Geographic Society, John M. Fahey, Jr., President and Chief
Executive Officer; Gilbert M. Grosvenor, Chairman of the Board;
Nina D. Hoffman, Executive Vice President and President, Books
and Education Publishing Group.

PREPARED BY NATIONAL GEOGRAPHIC SCHOOL PUBLISHING
Ericka Markman, Senior Vice President and President, Children's
Books and Education Publishing Group; Steve Mico, Vice President
and Editorial Director; Marianne Hiland, Executive Editor; Richard
Easby, Editorial Manager; Jim Hiscott, Design Manager; Kristin
Hanneman, Illustrations Manager; Matt Wascavage, Manager of
Publishing Services; Sean Philpotts, Production Manager.

EDITORIAL MANAGEMENT
Morrison BookWorks, LLC

PROGRAM CONSULTANTS
Dr. Shirley V. Dickson, Program Director, Literacy, Education
Commission of the States; Margit E. McGuire, Ph.D., Professor of
Teacher Education and Social Studies, Seattle University.

National Geographic Theme Sets program developed by Macmillan
Education Australia, Pty Limited.

Published by the National Geographic Society
1145 17th Street, N.W.
Washington, D.C. 20036-4688

ISBN: 07922-47434

Printed in Hong Kong.

2011 2010 2009 2008
5 6 7 8 9 10 11 12 13 14 15

Contents

Inventions Bring Change

New inventions play a big part in making life easier for people. The invention of trains and cars, for example, allowed people to travel quickly from place to place. Machines in factories made it easier to make clothes. Power stations offered new ways to get light and heat. The reaper, the railroad, water-powered mills, and the cotton gin are all inventions that changed people's lives.

 ## Key Concepts ....

1. Inventions, such as machines, are usually designed to solve problems and to get work done in a more efficient way.

2. Inventions often cause changes in people's daily lives.

3. Many inventions lead to the development of other inventions.

Four Kinds of Inventions

The Reaper

The reaper was invented to cut wheat more quickly.

The Railroad

The railroad moved goods and people farther and faster.

In this book you will learn about changes brought by the invention of the railroad.

Water Power

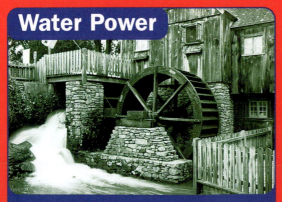

Water power was used to drive machines in mills.

The Cotton Gin

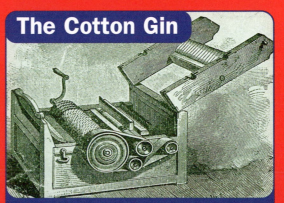

The cotton gin was invented to remove seeds from cotton.

The Railroad
Changed the West

Do you ever travel by train? Train travel allows you to get from one place to another quickly. Before **railroads** were invented, travel was much slower. During the nineteenth century, many people moved to the western region of the United States. The railroad played an important role in moving people to the West.

Moving to the West

At the beginning of the 1800s, most people in the United States lived in the East. Not many people had moved west of the Mississippi River. Explorers told people back in the East about the West. They said that not many people lived there.

Salt Lake City, in the western state of Utah, was a small town in 1850.

People in the East began to think about moving west. Many people wanted to own farmland. Others wanted to set up a store or other business. The West seemed like a good place to start a new life. But traveling to the West was very hard. The journey was very long and difficult. The railroad provided an easier way to travel.

Look at the map below to see where the West is located.

The West

WASHINGTON

MONTANA

OREGON

IDAHO

WYOMING

NEVADA

UTAH

COLORADO

CALIFORNIA

United States

Mississippi River

N
W E
S

0 mi   500
0 km   500

Key
Western states

Problems with Travel

Before there were trains, people used horses and carts to travel on land. To get to the West, people often went in **wagon trains**. A wagon train was a long line of wagons pulled by horses, oxen, or mules. It took the wagon trains many months to reach the West. The journey was dangerous and very hard. Many people died along the way.

Settlers were people who went to live in the West. They needed a faster, safer way of getting there. Then the settlers could start their farms or set up their businesses. The railroad to the West gave settlers the help they needed.

Wagon trains traveling west in the 1800s

Inventing the Railroad

The **invention** of the first railroad happened in Europe. Horses pulled a line of wagons along wooden rails. Cast-iron rails replaced wooden rails in the late eighteenth century.

By the 1860s, in the United States, steel rails replaced cast-iron rails. The steel rails did not rust. As a result, they lasted longer and worked in a more **efficient** way. Steel rails are still used today.

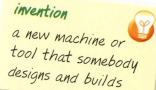

invention
a new machine or tool that somebody designs and builds

efficient
able to do more work in less time

A horse-drawn railroad car carrying goods and passengers

The First Locomotive

In 1829, an Englishman named Robert Stephenson invented the **locomotive**. A locomotive is the front section of a train that pulls the rest of the train. The first kind of locomotive was **powered** by a **machine** called a steam engine. Coal or wood was burned for power. Stephenson's locomotive, called the *Rocket*, had a top speed of 35 miles (56 kilometers) per hour.

machine
several moving parts working together to do a job

Robert Stephenson's *Rocket*

How the Railroad Works

The railroad uses a system of rails. Two steel rails lie next to each other. They are several feet apart but connected by ties. The ties are long wooden blocks that sit under the rails. They support the rails. Chairs and clips hold the rails in place.

The rail system carries the weight of the trains. Some trains are more than 1 mile (1.6 kilometers) long.

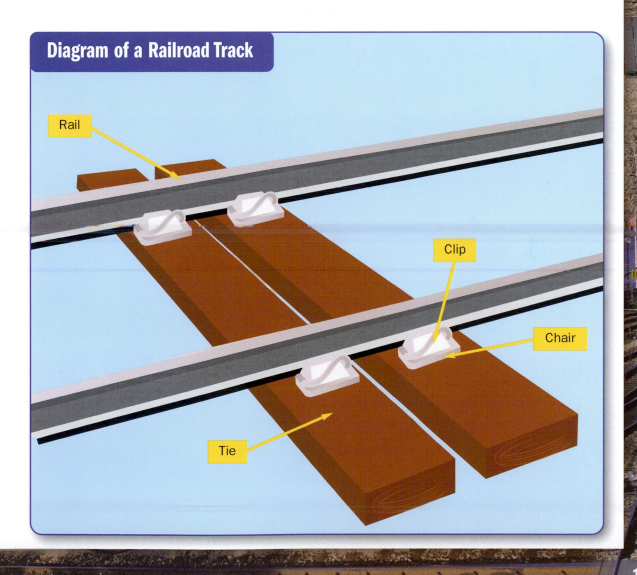

Diagram of a Railroad Track

Rail

Clip

Chair

Tie

The Railroad to the West

The growth of the American railroad opened up travel to the West. By the 1850s, people could travel by rail from New York to Chicago. Then they could go to the Missouri River, in Iowa. The tracks stopped there. People wanted a **transcontinental** railroad built. The railroad would join the East Coast to the West Coast.

Work on the transcontinental railroad started in 1863. The Central Pacific Railroad Company started building tracks east from California. The Union Pacific Railroad Company started building tracks west from the Missouri River. In 1869, the tracks met in Promontory Point, Utah. The finished railroad made travel easier and faster.

Replicas of the first transcontinental railroad locomotives at Promontory Point, Utah

How the Railroad Changed Lives

The railroad changed the lives of many people in the United States. The West was no longer cut off from the rest of the country. People could move west easily.

Direct Routes

Soon after the transcontinental railroad was built, other rail **routes** were built. These routes connected towns across the West. People could now travel by direct route to other towns and cities. Train travel was a safe way of moving around.

By train, mail could be delivered to other cities and towns in a few days. Mail became an easy way for people to keep in touch with family and friends across the United States.

A mail train carrying cargo across the Sierra Nevada Mountains in 1870

Development of Towns

Before the railroad, the West had few towns. But as railroad routes were being built, towns grew alongside them. Towns along a railroad route could get goods more easily than towns farther away. So people opened shops in these towns.

Farming in the West

People could now **transport** animals more easily. Many people set up farms in the West. They raised animals for meat and dairy products. These products could be transported to other towns by train and sold there.

Cattle are herded onto a train for shipment.

Other Inventions

The invention of the railroad led to other inventions in transport. Steam-powered locomotives moved the trains for many years. However, they were not ideal. The engines needed a lot of fuel. They also let out thick, black smoke. This smoke got passengers dirty. It bothered people who lived near the tracks.

Diesel Engines

Diesel engines began to replace steam engines after 1934. Diesel engines needed less fuel. They caused less pollution. Diesel engines could also go much faster. They were more reliable.

A new diesel train alongside an older, steam train in New York, 1937

Cars, Trucks, and Airplanes

Other means of transport were developed after the railroad. In 1885, Gottlieb Daimler and Karl Benz built the first gasoline car engines. By the early 1900s, many cars were being made. Trucks followed soon after. People could travel when and where they wanted in a car. Trucks could carry goods from place to place.

In 1903, Orville and Wilbur Wright built the first successful airplane. By the 1930s, airplanes were being used to transport people and goods.

Many people today use cars for transport.

Airplanes fly people and goods over long distances.

Think About the **Key Concepts**

Think about what you read. Think about the pictures and the diagram. Use these to answer the questions. Share what you think with others.

1. What are some problems that inventions have helped to solve?

2. Besides solving problems, what are some other reasons that people invent things like machines?

3. What are some effects of inventions on people's lives?

4. Give some examples of inventions that have led to the development of other inventions.

Labeled Diagram

A labeled diagram is a picture of something with the parts labeled.

A labeled diagram of a machine shows you the different parts that make up the machine. You can see how the machine works by seeing how the different parts work together.

Look back at the labeled diagram on page 11. It is a diagram of a railroad track. The diagram on page 19 is also a labeled diagram. It shows you the different parts that make up a steam locomotive.

How to Read a Diagram

1. **Read the title.**
   The title tells you what machine the diagram shows.

2. **Study the picture.**
   The picture shows you what the machine looks like.

3. **Read the labels.**
   The labels tell you the names of the parts and what they are used for.

4. **Think about how the machine works.**
   See if you can figure out how the different parts of the machine work together.

Diagram of a Steam Locomotive

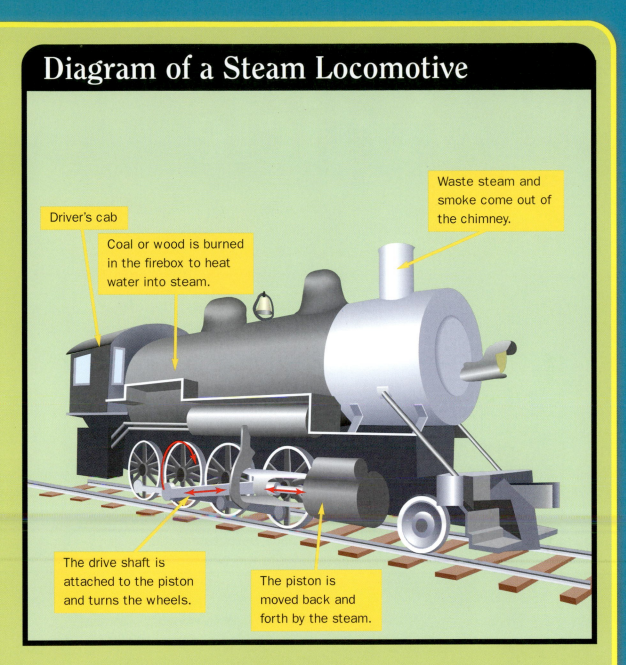

Driver's cab

Coal or wood is burned in the firebox to heat water into steam.

Waste steam and smoke come out of the chimney.

The drive shaft is attached to the piston and turns the wheels.

The piston is moved back and forth by the steam.

How Does It Work?

Read the diagram by following the steps on page 18. What did you find out about how a steam locomotive works? Describe what you learned to a classmate. See if your classmate understands the diagram the same way you do.

Compare-Contrast Article

A **compare-contrast article** shows how two people, places, things, or events are alike and different. The article beginning on page 21 compares and contrasts life in the United States before and after the building of the transcontinental railroad.

A compare-contrast article usually contains the following:

An **introduction** that focuses on the topic and outlines the main points to be compared and contrasted

Several **body paragraphs** that discuss ways the two topics are alike and ways they are different from one another

Clue words throughout the article that highlight likenesses and differences

A **conclusion** that ties ideas together

The United States
Before and After
the Transcontinental Railroad

The **title** identifies the topic of the article.

Life in the American West changed a great deal after the transcontinental railroad was developed. Before the railroad, travel was slow and uncomfortable, and moving west was a challenge. It was hard to transport goods overland. After the railroad, people's ideas about where they could live changed. Towns and businesses grew, but the Native Americans suffered as a result. The railroad changed the way of life in the western United States.

The **introduction** outlines the main points that will be compared and contrasted.

Photographs, **illustrations**, or diagrams may make ideas clearer.

A steam locomotive chugs down the tracks of the transcontinental railroad.

Before the Railroad

Before the railroad, travel was difficult. It was hard to move goods from place to place. It took people a long time to get anywhere. Horse-drawn carriages, called stagecoaches, carried people over long distances. However, traveling in stagecoaches was very slow. The coaches had to stop many times along the way. The drivers had to feed and rest or change the horses. The horses could carry or pull only small loads. So people could not take much with them.

Before the railroad, poor roads made travel difficult. Roads were usually not paved, and in some places they flooded often. Many roads were too steep for horses to get up easily. The roads made traveling by wagon uncomfortable and risky.

Clue words highlight likenesses and differences.

Body paragraphs near the beginning of the article describe life before the invention.

A stagecoach traveling in South Dakota

This painting shows Native Americans hunting bison before railroads brought settlers to the West.

Before the railroad came, most towns and cities were built near water. This was because people could travel easily by barge or steamboat. Towns with seaports had an advantage compared to towns without seaports. Towns located along waterways could grow and flourish because travel in and out was easier.

Before the railroad, there were many Native American communities in the West. The Great Plains had huge herds of bison. Native Americans hunted the bison for food, clothing, and most of the things they needed.

After the Railroad

Clue words highlight likenesses and differences.

After the railroad was built, travel from east to west became much faster and easier. The old ways of traveling were slow, dangerous, and cost a great deal of money.

Body paragraphs that come later in the article describe life after the invention.

With the railroad, people could travel where they wanted, when they wanted. Instead of moving slowly, they could travel quickly and comfortably.

The railroad also changed the way people moved goods. They could now move large amounts of goods instead of only small amounts. As a result, industry spread. People could set up stores and businesses in more places.

After the railroad went west, towns no longer had to be built along waterways. They sprang up wherever the railroad went. People could set up stores the same as those in cities in the East. It was easier and quicker to move goods by train than by water.

A train on Devil's Gate Bridge in Georgetown, Colorado during the building of the transcontinental railroad

The railroad helped people transport their goods quickly and cheaply over long distances. Goods from the West could be carried to towns in the East. Goods from the East could get to the West.

As the new railroad moved across the United States, the Native Americans fought to keep their land. The railroad companies wanted to kill off the bison. They said the animals damaged the tracks and other railroad property.

Hunters killed millions of bison. Without bison to hunt, and with thousands of settlers arriving, Native Americans lost their traditional way of life.

A group of men shoot bison from the top of a railroad train.

A Life-Changing Invention

The **conclusion** summarizes the likenesses and differences.

After the transcontinental railroad was built, many people's lives changed. Thousands of people traveled by railroad to make their homes in the Great Plains and the West. Native American culture was almost wiped out.

The landscape was also changed as cities grew along the railroad. The railroad brought a time of great growth and change for the United States.

Railroad workers celebrating the completion of the transcontinental railroad on May 10, 1869

Apply the Key Concepts

Key Concept 1 Inventions, such as machines, are usually designed to solve problems and to get work done in a more efficient way.

Activity

Think of all the problems that the invention of the railroad solved. Create a word web to show the problems. Then write a sentence that summarizes the word web. Use the word *efficient* in your sentence.

slow travel

Problems Before the Railroad

Key Concept 2 Inventions often cause changes in people's daily lives.

Activity

Write a list of the ways people's lives changed because of the invention of the railroad. Next to each change, write whether you think the change was good or bad.

How Lives Changed

1.
2.
3.
4.

Key Concept 3 Many inventions lead to the development of other inventions.

Activity

Draw a short timeline to show the inventions that followed the railroad. Include a brief description of each invention.

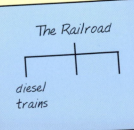

The Railroad

diesel trains

RESEARCH AND WRITE

Write Your Own
Compare-Contrast Article

You have read the article that compares and contrasts life before and after the railroad. Now you are going to write your own compare-contrast article.

1. Study the Model

Look back at the description of compare-contrast writing on page 20. Then read the article again. Notice that the first body paragraphs tell about "before" the railroad. Write down the main point of each of these paragraphs. Then look at the "after" paragraphs. Write down the main point of each of these paragraphs. Notice that the main points in the "before" and "after" sections are alike.

Writing a Compare-Contrast Article

◆ Choose a topic with several likenesses and differences.

◆ Write an introduction that focuses your topic.

◆ Cover the same main points in the "before" paragraphs and in the "after" paragraphs.

◆ Use clue words to highlight likenesses and differences.

◆ Tie your ideas together in your conclusion.

2. Choose Your Topic

Now choose an invention that you would like to find out more about. Look on the Internet or in books about inventions to get some ideas. Choose an invention that made a big change in people's lives.

3. Research Your Topic

Do research to find out more about the invention. Why was there a need for the invention? What are several ways that the invention changed people's lives? Were these changes all good, or were some bad? Make notes on what you find out. You may need to use several sources to find the information you need.

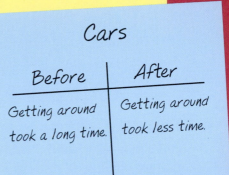

Cars

Before	After
Getting around took a long time.	Getting around took less time.

4. Write a Draft

Organize your notes so that each main point in the "before" section matches up with a main point in the "after" section. Then begin writing. Be sure to include an introduction that focuses your article and a conclusion that brings your ideas together.

5. Revise and Edit

Once you have finished writing, check over your article. Make sure that the "before" and "after" sections have about the same amount of information. Correct any spelling or punctuation errors.

Create a Group Photograph Album

Now that you have written your compare-contrast article, you can share what you learned with the class. With a group of students, you can make a photograph album showing how the invention you researched changed people's lives.

How to Make a Photograph Album

1. Find the photographs.
Look back over your research. Look for photographs you can print from the Internet or photocopy from a book. The photographs should show life before the invention and life after the invention.

2. Paste your photographs onto paper.
Paste the "before" photographs onto one piece of paper and the "after" photographs onto another piece of paper.

3. Write captions for your photographs.
Your captions should explain what is happening in the photographs.

4. Bind the pages together in a group album.
Put the pages in order so that the "before" photographs face the "after" photographs. Tie the pages together with yarn and include a cardboard cover. Put a title on the cover that tells how the photographs are connected.

5. Share your albums with the class.
Put all the albums at the front of the classroom, along with the compare-contrast articles. Take time to review the albums.

Glossary

efficient – able to do more work in less time

invention – a new machine or tool that somebody designs and builds

locomotive – the front section of a train that pulls the rest of the train

machine – several moving parts working together to do a job

powered – driven, or made to work

railroads – parallel steel tracks and the trains that move along them

routes – different paths or ways of getting somewhere

settlers – people who move from one place to start a new community in another place

transcontinental – crossing a continent

transport – the carrying of people or goods from one place to another

wagon trains – a long line of covered wagons pulled by horses, oxen, or mules

Index